Arts & Crafts

STENCILS
AND SCREENS

Susie O'Reilly
With photographs by Zul Mukhida

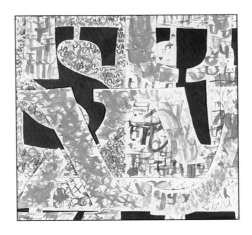

Thomson Learning
New York

Titles in this series

BATIK AND TIE-DYE
BLOCK PRINTING
MODELING
PAPERMAKING
STENCILS AND SCREENS
WEAVING

Frontispiece *Alphabet stencils
designed and cut by schoolchildren
with the help of letterer David
Holgate.*

First published in the
United States in 1993 by
Thomson Learning
115 Fifth Avenue
New York, NY 10003

First published in 1993 by
Wayland (Publishers) Ltd.

Library of Congress Cataloging-in-Publication Data
O'Reilly, Susie, 1949–
  Stencils and screens / Susie O'Reilly ; with photographs by
Zul Mukhida
      p.   cm. — (Arts & crafts)
  Includes bibliographical references and index.
  ISBN 1-56847-068-1 : $14.95
  1. Stencil work — Juvenile literature. 2. Screen process
printing — Juvenile literature. [1. Stencil work. 2. Screen
process printing. 3. Handicraft.] I. Mukhida, Zul, ill. II. Title.
III. Series.
TT270.074   1994
745.7'3 — dc20   93-28349

Printed in Italy.

CONTENTS

Words printed in **bold** appear in the glossary.

GETTING STARTED

Stenciling and screen printing are both simple ways of applying color and pattern to a surface. Using these processes, you can make patterns that repeat the same **motif** over and over, or you can make a number of identical prints. In both **techniques** certain areas of a design are masked out to block the color from reaching the print surface, while the unmasked areas let the color through.

Stenciling is one of the oldest of all decorative techniques. It has been used since the **Stone Age**, although it didn't get its name until the fifteenth century. The word "stencil" comes from the medieval French word "estenceler," which means to sparkle. That is a good way to describe the lively, light effect of a stenciled pattern.

Screen printing is put to all sorts of uses. This man is printing a poster. ▶

▼ *Stencil brushes have short, stubby bristles.*

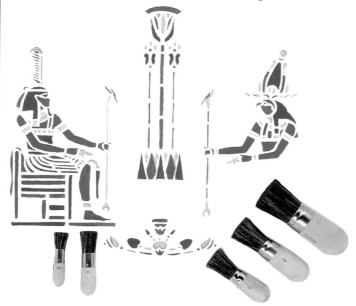

Screen printing is a development of stenciling. In screen printing, ink is forced through a screen onto a flat surface. The masking lies between the screen and the material being printed. The first screens were made of silk, so the technique was called silk screen printing. Now the mesh is usually made of cotton or **synthetic** material rather than silk.

Objects made in a wide range of materials, including paper, cardboard, wood, metal, plaster, glass, plastic, pottery, and cloth, can be decorated with screen printed and stenciled designs. Stenciling is mainly a hand process used by artists and craftspeople. Screen printing can be done by hand or machine by artists, skilled printers, or factory workers using computer-driven equipment. Screen printing is used on many everyday items, including posters, price tags, tickets, clothes, curtains, tiles, teakettles, toasters, wallpaper, and dishes.

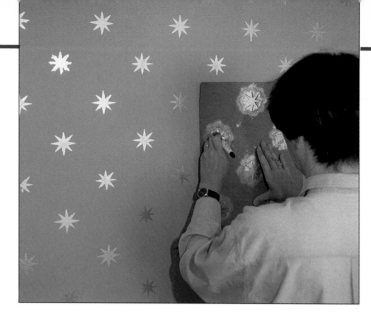

▲ *Stenciling can be used to decorate a wall.*

To get started you will need these tools and materials.

General equipment:
Paper and cardboard
Cloth (plain cotton is best)
Masking tape
Clear tape
Newspapers
Paper tissues and towels
Craft knife
Cutting board
Scissors
Tracing paper
Metal ruler
Iron
Old plastic bowl
Rubber gloves
Apron
Pencils
Fine sandpaper
Waterproof varnish
Notebook

For stenciling:
Oiled stencil paper (from an arts and craft store)
Thin cardboard (poster board works well)
Vegetable oil
Stencil brushes with short stubby hairs (from an arts and craft store)
Pieces of sponge
Quick-drying paints (e.g., poster and acrylic paints)

For screen printing:
Wooden frames (old picture frames are ideal)
Fine nylon mesh (e.g., old nylon net curtains)
Thumbtacks and a small hammer
Brown paper packing tape
Newsprint
Screen printing ink and binder (from a crafts store) or lead-free wallpaper paste to add to poster paint
A **squeegee** (a plastic ruler, strip of cardboard or vinyl floor tile, or window or windshield wiper)
An old spoon
Cold-water dyes (e.g., Deka cold-water dyes)

STENCILING AROUND THE WORLD

Stenciling is an ancient art form that has been used by people all over the world. Early stencilers used whatever materials came to hand. Some examples of early stenciled patterns can still be seen, but the stencils themselves have not survived. Either they wore out or they disintegrated over time.

Examples of early stenciling can be found in some rock and cave paintings. The cave artists discovered that they could make an image by spraying color through a hollow bone or plant stalk around the spread fingers of their hands. In this way, their own hands acted as very simple stencils.

In prehistoric times cave artists used their hands as stencils. These very old rock paintings are in Mexico. ▶

▼ *Blue* adire *cloth from West Africa*

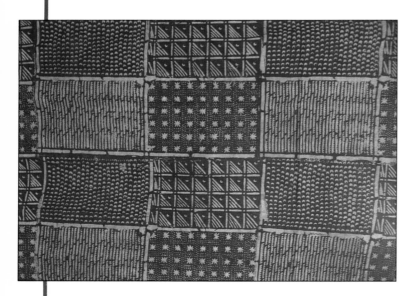

On Fiji, in the Pacific Ocean, the islanders traditionally decorate their clothing with simple stencils cut from bamboo and banana leaves. In west Africa, the Yoruba people use stencils to make *adire* cloth, which has light blue and white designs on a blue background. They use sheets of pierced tin to apply patterns of flour paste onto cotton cloth before the cloth is put into dark blue dye. The dye does not color the areas covered by paste. The Inuit people on Baffin Island in the Arctic use stencils cut from dried sealskin.

◄ *Japanese robes stenciled with bold designs*

A stenciled ▶ *bedroom in a house in Connecticut*

Both the Japanese and Chinese have used stenciling for centuries. The Japanese discovered a way of making strong, **durable** stencils out of paper made from mulberry bush bark and waterproofed with a coating of **persimmon** juice. In the sixth and seventh centuries they decorated the leather armor of their **samurai warriors** with stenciled decorations. By the nineteenth century, they had discovered a way to hold the different parts of a stencil together with a web of silk threads and human hair. They used these delicate stencils to print intricate pictures and patterns on fine silk.

The early European settlers in North America could not afford to carpet their floors, paper their walls, or import fine furniture, so they used stenciling to decorate their houses.

In North America, ▶ *stenciling was a popular way of brightening simple furniture. This American rocking chair dates from the early nineteenth century.*

Some people did their own stenciling, but it was more common to hire a decorator. These artists traveled from town to town working for anyone who could afford their fees. They stenciled flowers, leaves, stars, birds, bells, and pineapples in warm, earthy colors over pale gray, red, or dark blue backgrounds. In 1818 Lambert Hitchcock set up a furniture stenciling factory in the small town of Barkhamsted, Connecticut. The work of his stencilers, many of whom were women, become so well known that the town was nicknamed Hitchcockville.

By World War II, simpler interiors came into fashion and stenciling fell out of fashion. Recently, however, there has been a great revival of the craft in Europe and North America. Stenciling is now seen as an art form and has been used to decorate expensive restaurants and hotels. Many people are again using stenciling in their homes.

CUTTING STENCILS

A good stencil design consists of clean, bold shapes. The spaces between the shapes are as important as the shapes themselves. Use thin cardboard to make your stencils. You can buy special stencil cardboard from an arts and crafts store, or you can use thin cardboard – poster board is about the right thickness.

2 Make an accurate drawing of your design, then trace it onto tracing paper.

1 Experiment with a design on pieces of scrap paper. Turn to pages 26-29 for some ideas for designs and for advice on how to use these ideas to make stencils. Allow for good **bridges** of cardboard between the cutout spaces. This makes not only a good design but also a strong stencil that will not break up in use. Leave at least a 5-inch margin all around the outside of the design so that the brush will not smudge paint over the edge when you are stenciling.

3 Tape the tracing firmly to the stencil cardboard with masking tape.

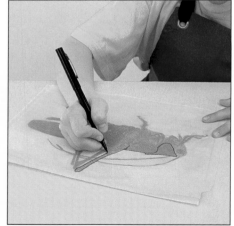

4 Now cut out the design, cutting through the tracing paper and the cardboard. Use a cutting board and a sharp craft knife. **Remember: Always be careful when using a craft knife. Ask an adult to help you. Use even pressure as you cut.**

6 If you are using ordinary cardboard, wipe a thin layer of vegetable oil over your stencil with a paper towel. Let the oil dry. Oiling the cardboard makes it stronger and more **flexible**. You do not need to oil stencil cardboard, since it has been oiled already.

5 Start by cutting out the smallest spaces in your design. The cardboard becomes weaker as more shapes are cut out, so you will have difficulty cutting fine shapes if you leave them until last.

7 If you tear one of the bridges of your stencil, repair it with a piece of clear tape.

8 When you have finished stenciling, store your stencil flat in a folder.

MAKING A STENCILED PRINT

A well-stenciled print has sharp, crisp outlines and soft, rich colors built up in layers. It is worth taking your time when stenciling to make sure you get a good result.

1 Place the object to be stenciled on a table covered with a layer of newspaper.

2 Think carefully about how you will position the stencil. The spaces above and below will play an important part in how it looks.

3 Tape the stencil to the surface with masking tape (masking tape can be peeled off afterward and will not leave a mark).

4 Pour some paint into a saucer. If possible, use a white saucer so that you can see the color of the paint. Use quick-drying paint such as poster or acrylic paint. If you prefer, you can buy special fast-drying stencil paint from an arts and crafts store.

5 Dip your stenciling brush into the paint. Then dab it on a paper towel or newspaper to get rid of any excess paint. If you have too much paint on the brush it will run under the edges of the stencil.

7 When you have finished stenciling, remove all the masking tape from the stencils and gently wipe them clean. Wash the brushes out thoroughly and let them dry, bristles up.

6 Hold the brush like a pencil, keeping it upright, with your fingers close to the bristles. Work the brush in broad, circular movements, clockwise and counterclockwise, until the shapes are gradually filled in. Build up the color slowly by applying several layers. Do not try to get a thick, rich effect using lots of paint all at once. You can also dab on the paint with pieces of sponge.

▼ *Use stencils to make a repeating pattern – like that of some wallpaper.*

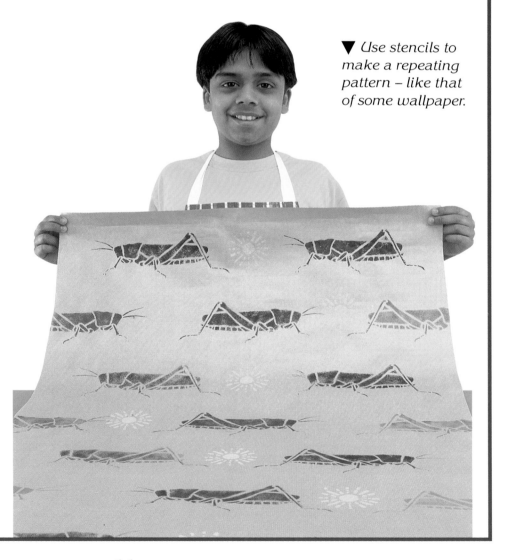

MAKING A MULTICOLORED PRINT

A multicolored design can be built up using several stencils and printing with different colored paints. A detailed design can be made in this way.

1 Draw a design using three colors and three stencils. The first stencil should give the main outline and background of the pattern. The second and third stencils should add detail.

2 If your design involves printing one color on top of another, choose the palest color for the first stencil and the darkest color for the last.

3 Make a tracing for each color and cut out the three stencils.

4 Check that the stencils line up. Place each one in turn on top of another, and draw each outline onto each of the other stencils. Use pencil. If all three do not line up, try again until the outline for each stencil is correctly positioned.

5 Place all the stencils on top of one another, making sure each one matches its pencil outline. Cut out small triangles at the top, bottom, and sides, cutting through all three stencils to make identical marks. These will be your **registration marks** and will help you position each stencil correctly.

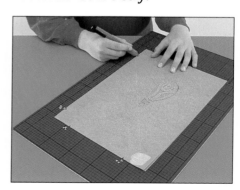

6 Stick the first stencil on a piece of paper with masking tape. Use a pencil to trace the triangular registration marks.

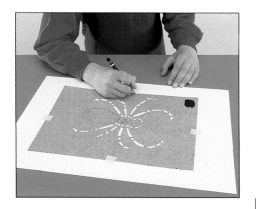

7 Use paint to make a print through the first stencil. Let the paint dry.

8 Position the second stencil over the print. Move it around until all the registration marks show. This means the second stencil is in the correct position.

9 Make a print from the second stencil and let the paint dry.

10 Now line up the third stencil with the registration marks and print.

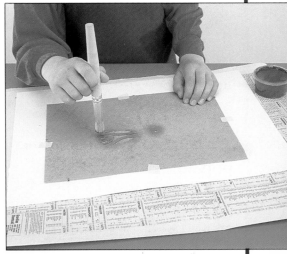

THE HISTORY OF SCREEN PRINTING

Screen printing is a very important printing technique. It has been used widely by businesses and industry, as well as by artists, since its discovery about a hundred years ago. In the 1870s, experiments were made to find a method making a stencil on a screen made of silk. The idea grew, and in 1907 Englishman Samuel Simon applied for a **patent** for his technique of silk screen printing. At first, screen printing was used mainly by the **textile** industry to print patterned cloth quickly and cheaply. Soon the advertising, packaging, and labeling industries started to use it to **mass-produce** banners, posters, cards, and labels.

◄ *Screens can be used to hand print designs onto fabric.*

At first, a paper stencil was attached to the underside of the screen. Later on, areas of the screen were painted with a varnish that would block the printing ink. Both of these methods are still used by some hand screen printers today.

Around 1916, another method was developed. The screen was coated with a **gelatin** that was sensitive to light. Parts of the screen were then exposed to light. The gelatin hardened in the parts that the light reached, but could be washed away from the unexposed parts. The hardened gelatin acted like a stencil when ink was wiped over the screen.

At first, artists were reluctant to use the new technique of screen printing because a screen print was so unlike a painting. With paint and brushes they could create detailed and textured paintings, but screen printing produced bold, simple designs, with plain colors and clean, crisp edges.

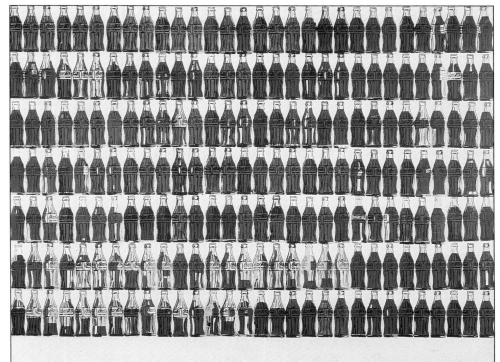

Screen printing was not widely used by artists until the 1960s. The American painter Andy Warhol used it to make different prints of series of identical images. Each print in a series was in a different **color scheme.** He had been using rubber stamps, but realized that screen printing offered an ideal method of producing these "multiples." People were shocked by his prints of Coca-Cola bottles and Campbell's soup cans. They weren't used to seeing everyday objects as subjects for works of art. However, many painters followed Warhol's example and started to use screen printing in their work. Over the next thirty years screen printing developed as an important **medium** for artists.

▲ *Andy Warhol's* Green Coca-Cola bottle *(1962)*

▲ Green Dominance *(1977) by Bridget Riley. The artist uses screen printing to produce clean, crisp lines in her work.*

"Futurism" at Lenabo *(1964) by Eduardo Paolozzi. A different screen is used for each color. How many different colors can you count?* ▶

MAKING A SCREEN

Frames for screen printing are sold at arts and crafts stores. You can make your own frame from strips of wood, or use a cardboard box with a hole cut in the bottom. One of the best ways to start is to find a sturdy old picture frame with **rigid** corners.

1 Cut a piece of fine-mesh nylon netting a little larger than your frame.

2 Wet the nylon and stretch it over the frame as tightly as possible.

3 Pin the mesh to the frame with thumbtacks. Start at the center of one side and work a couple of inches to either side, keeping the tacks close together. On the opposite side of the frame, pull the nylon as tightly as you can and put tacks in it across from your first tacks.

4 Do not finish either side yet. Pin the remaining two sides in the same way. Now work along each of the sides to the corners, pulling the nylon as tightly and evenly as you can. **Ask an adult to help you with the hammer and tacks.**

5 Let the nylon dry. As it dries it will shrink. The screen must be stretched as tight as a drum, with no wrinkles.

6 Trim the extra netting from the edges of the screen. Then paste a layer of waterproof glue over the edges of the frame.

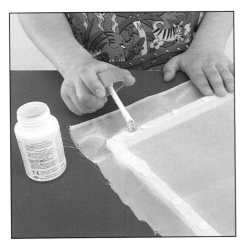

Cut four strips of packing tape. Trim them to size, wet them, and use them to mask the inside edges of the screen.

7 Lay the screen on the table with the mesh face up. Use brown paper packing tape to mask the edges of the screen. Wet the tape in a bowl of water before sticking it to the screen.

8 Now turn the screen over so that the mesh is facedown on the table.

This will keep the printing ink from spreading under the edge of the frame. It will also serve as the **reservoir** in which the pool of ink is held before it is pulled across the screen.

9 If you want to make a large number of prints it is a good idea to paint waterproof varnish over the tape.

10 Clean the varnish off the brush using paint thinner.

11 If the packing tape starts to lift, use fresh strips to restick the edges of the screen and cover them with varnish.

MAKING A SCREEN PRINT

1 Cover a table with an old, soft cloth or blanket. Over this, lay strips of plastic wrap covered with newspapers. Place a thick pad of newspaper in the center of the table.

2 Cut a paper stencil from a sheet of newsprint. Turn to pages 26-27 for information on designing stencils.

3 Now prepare your printing ink. Mix up some lead-free wallpaper paste powder with water. Use half the water suggested on the packet so that the paste is quite thick. Wait until it becomes a clear jelly. Then add some poster paint or some dye powder dissolved in hot water. You can also buy screen printing ink and binder (pictured below).

4 Find a squeegee. You can use a window wiper, a flexible plastic ruler, or a strip of vinyl floor tile. The squeegee must be slightly shorter than the width of the screen, but long enough to cover your design.

5 Now practice making a print. Put a test piece of printing paper on the newspaper pad. Put the stencil on the paper and place the screen over the stencil.

6 Spoon some of your printing ink onto the packing tape reservoir at the side of the screen.

7 Ask a friend to hold the screen firmly on the table. Using your squeegee, pull the ink across the screen toward you. A good print has the same strength of color throughout. It is made by sweeping the correct amount of ink across the screen in one even, nonstop movement. This takes practice.

8 Lift the screen off the print (the stencil will stick to the screen). Place the print on a flat surface to dry.

9 Make a second test print. You will probably find that the first prints are not very good. They will get better as the paper stencil adheres to the wet ink.

10 Now make your actual print in exactly the same way. You can print on paper or cloth. You can also make a number of prints from the screen. Keep your printing area tidy by removing any inky paper from your newspaper pad after each print.

11 When you have finished printing, wash the ink off the screen while it is still wet. Use dishwashing liquid and a soft cloth.

If you let the ink dry on the screen it will clog up the holes in the mesh and you will not be able to use it again. Make sure you do not wash away the tape on the edges. Leave the screen standing on its side to dry.

SCREEN PRINTING A T-SHIRT

There is no limit to the range of designs you can screen print on a T-shirt. You might print your name or the name of a famous person, a funny slogan, or simply an attractive pattern. You can use different screens to print different parts of the T-shirt.

1 Find a plain, light-colored T-shirt. If it is new, wash it to get rid of the **finish**. The finish might keep the cloth from soaking up the ink.

2 Cut a piece of cardboard the size of the body of the T-shirt and slip it inside. This will keep the ink from soaking through to the back of the shirt when you print on the front.

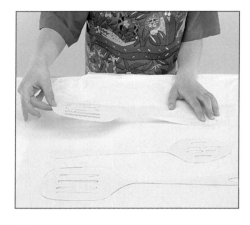

3 Prepare your paper stencils.

TURN TO PAGES 26-27 FOR INFORMATION ON DESIGNING STENCILS.

TURN TO PAGES 18-19 FOR INFORMATION ON SCREEN PRINTING.

4 Place the T-shirt on your printing pad and screen print your design. You will need to use screen-printing ink made for fabric. You can also use a cold-water dye, such as Deka, mixed with a textile binder from a crafts store.

5 When the T-shirt is dry, iron it with a cool iron to fix the color. **Ask an adult to help you use the iron.**

Remember: Your T-shirt must be washed separately. Some of the color might run and stain other clothes.

▼ *Two T-shirt designs based on the same idea: the blue one uses a positive image and the red one a negative image (see page 26).*

CUTTING AN ALPHABET STENCIL

Letters make good stencils because they are strong, simple shapes. Alphabet stencils are often used to spray names and instructions on labels and packing crates. You can label things with an alphabet stencil, or you can use it to make a collage.

1 Start by collecting examples of different letter shapes. Look at magazines and newspapers, posters, shopping bags, boxes, food packets, and signs. Look at the cover of this book. You will discover that there are lots of different ways to form letters.

2 Another way to find a variety of letters is to print out the alphabet in different **fonts** on a word processor.

3 Choose some of the letters and use a photocopier to enlarge them.

4 Design and cut stencils using the enlarged letters as the basis of your design. Trace the shapes with tracing paper. Think about the bridges you will need.

5 Different designs can be used to stencil the same letter. Experiment with the shapes. For example, the picture above shows ten different ways to stencil the letter "O."

6 Design the other letters of the alphabet and cut stencils for them. There are twenty-six letters, so ask some friends to help you.

8 Another idea is to make just a few letters and use them to make a picture. You can stencil the letters any way you like – on their sides, or at an angle. Experiment and have fun.

7 If you want to write words for labels, make sure you position each letter carefully next to the one before, so that they are in a straight line.

DECORATING A BOX

Stenciling is an ideal way to decorate a box. Boxes have three **dimensions**, so there are many surfaces to decorate. They can be picked up and turned around to give different views. The box will be opened and sometimes people will look underneath it. You need to think about how the outside and the inside decoration will look. You also need to think about what the box is going to contain. You can make the design tell something about the contents, or about the person who will own the box.

2 Decide on a stencil design for the box and make the stencils you will need.

3 Strip off any paper labels. Use fine sandpaper to rub the box down. The wood needs to be smooth all over.

1 Find a small wooden box – a cigar, cheese, or stationery box will be ideal.

> **Be careful not to breathe in any dust.**

4 Paint an undercoat on the wood using poster paint. The paint must cover the box smoothly and not let any old markings show through.

5 Once the paint is dry, sand the box again lightly. Brush off the dust. Then give the wood a second undercoat.

6 Before you start stenciling, try putting the stencils in different positions. This will help you decide where to place them to create the best effect.

7 Stencil the design on the box.

8 Add extra decorative details using a paintbrush if you wish.

9 Give the box several coats of varnish. Let the varnish dry and sand lightly between each coat.

DESIGNING STENCILS

A stenciled design is made up of **positive** shapes
(the areas that are cut out to take the paint) and **negative** shapes
(the areas that block the paint). In a good design, these shapes and
the bridges that hold the stencil in one piece look good together.

DESIGNING A STENCIL

4 Trace over the sketch. Try to improve the shapes, making the outlines crisper.

5 Trace over your tracing. Keep working on the design until you are really pleased with it. When you have cut out the stencil you can get an idea of how it will look when it is printed by placing it on a plain, colored background.

1 Find some ideas for your design (see pages 28-29). Try a simple design first.

2 Think carefully about which details will make positive shapes and which will make negative shapes. It is important to spend some time deciding where the bridges need to go and how wide to make them. The bridges add strength to the stencil and hold together parts of the design, but they must also blend in with the overall design.

3 Make a sketch. Try to make each shape as bold as possible.

26

MAKING A QUICK STENCIL

This method works for square, rectangular, and round stencils.

1 Fold a piece of paper in four.

2 Cut or tear pieces from the sides.

3 Unfold the paper.

MAKING A MORE COMPLICATED STENCIL

This method works for square or round stencils.

1 Fold a piece of paper in four, and then again, diagonally, into a triangle.

2 Draw a pattern on the triangle of paper.

3 Cut out the pattern. Be careful not to cut along the fold lines or your stencil will fall apart.

4 Unfold the paper.

THE GALLERY

All kinds of natural, handmade, and **manufactured** objects can give you ideas for stenciling and screen printing. Keep your camera or sketchbook ready to record things that have a good strong **silhouette,** or are made up of strong blocks of even color. Shapes that can be simplified easily make good stencil designs. Flowers, plants, and insects make good subjects for stencils because it is easy to blend the bridges into the overall design. While you are looking at shapes, make a note of which colors go well together, too.

▲ *Stripy zebra skins*

◀ *Apples with big shadows*

▼ *The silhouette of a tractor*

▲ Leaf shapes against the sky

▼ The pattern of a carved window

▲ Laundry drying on a line

A dahlia flower ▶

▼ Stork silhouettes and their reflections

GLOSSARY

Bridges In stencil making, the areas of cardboard holding the different parts of the design together. They are usually narrow strips of cardboard between the main, bold shapes of the design.

Color scheme In printing, the same design can be printed in a number of different color combinations. Each of these is called a color scheme.

Dimensions The amount of space an object takes up. A three-dimensional object has height, depth, and width.

Durable Long-lasting.

Finish The special surface put on cloth when it is made. It changes the way the cloth looks and feels.

Flexible Able to bend without breaking or cracking.

Font A complete set of type – the alphabet, numbers, symbols, and so on – that is all in the same style and size.

Gelatin A substance made by boiling animal bones. It is used in food to make jelly and in glue to make it sticky.

Manufactured Made in large quantities, usually by machines in a factory.

Mass-produce To manufacture a large quantity of the same object.

Medium A type of art, such as screen printing or sculpture or photography, that can be described by the particular techniques and materials used. Works of art are often grouped according to the medium in which they have been made.

Motif A shape, usually quite small, that is repeated to make a pattern.

Negative The opposite of positive. In a stencil design, the negative is the area of cardboard that blocks the paint.

Newsprint The special name for the type of low-quality paper that newspapers are printed on.

Patent A legal document that gives an inventor the right to use his invention and prevents other people from using it.

Persimmon A fruit that grows in tropical parts of the world.

Positive The opposite of negative. In a stencil design, the positive is the shape cut out to form the pattern. It is the area that lets the paint through.

Registration marks Marks that show a printer how to position a printing plate or stencil correctly. They are used when printing a design with more than one color. The registration marks for each color are lined up so that all the parts of the design fit together properly.

Reservoir An area that holds liquid. In screen printing, it is the part of the screen that holds the ink.

Rigid Unable to move; stiff.

Samurai warriors The fierce soldiers who formed the armies of Japan until the nineteenth century.

Silhouette The outline of a solid figure.

Squeegee A special tool used in screen printing to sweep ink evenly across the screen.

Stone Age A period of history many thousands of years ago. It is called the Stone Age because the early people of this time used stones to make tools.

Symmetrical Having two halves that are mirror images of each other.

Synthetic Made from chemicals; not natural.

Techniques Methods or skills.

Textiles All kinds of cloth, or the threads used to make cloth.

FURTHER INFORMATION

BOOKS TO READ

Nichols, Frank. *Stencils.* (New York: Child's Play International, 1989).

O'Reilly, Susie. *Block Printing.* Arts & Crafts. (New York: Thomson Learning, 1993).

For further information about arts and crafts, contact the following organization:

American Crafts Council
72 Spring Street
New York, NY 10012

Tofts, Hannah. *The Print Book.* (New York: Simon & Schuster, 1990).

Readers Digest Crafts & Hobbies (Pleasantville, N.Y. 1979).

INDEX

ACKNOWLEDGMENTS

The publishers would like to thank the following for allowing their photographs to be reproduced: American Museum in Britain 7 bottom; Bridgeman Art Library 7 top right, 15 all; Crafts Council *frontispiece* (E. Barber); Eye Ubiquitous 5 (P. Seheult), 7 top left (F. Leather), 14, 29 inset center (J. Stephens); Hutchison Library 6 left (J. Highet Brimah); Tony Stone Worldwide 28 left (P. McArthur); Topham 4 left; Zefa 4 right, 6 right, 28 top right (F. Lanting), 28 bottom right (B.

Peterson), 29 top left, 29 top right (R. Minsart), 29 bottom left, 29 bottom right (F. Lanting). All other photographs were supplied by Zul Mukhida. Logo artwork was supplied by John Yates.

The print *Green Dominance* (1977), by Bridget Riley, on page 15, appears by kind permission of the artist. The print *Green Coca-Cola bottle* (1962), by Andy Warhol, on page 15, appears by permission of the copyright holders: © 1993 The Andy Warhol Foundation for

the Visual Arts Inc. The publishers have made every attempt to contact the artist Eduardo Paolozzi for permission to reproduce the print *"Futurism" at Lenabo* (1964) on page 15.

The publishers would like to thank Shirley Chubb for providing the screen print photographed for the cover border and endpapers.

The author would like to thank Jan Peek, Jackie Lee, and Sarah Mossop for their help.